Nigel Marven's

# ANIMAL VAMPIRES

Out of the corner of my eye I saw something move. Another leech was only thirty centimetres away! Dangling from the tip of a tree-fern frond, it stretched hungrily towards me. To get it even more excited I breathed on it. The leech gently balanced on its rear sucker and swayed, probing the air like a blind man tapping a cane. This close, the leech could probably make out my shape. I looked down and realized I was surrounded. Leeches were approaching from all sides. Two were climbing from my sandles on to my toes and another three were searching for a feeding site on my shin.

# Nigel Marven's
# ANIMAL
# VAMPIRES

■SCHOLASTIC

Scholastic Children's Books
Commonwealth House, 1-19 New Oxford Street
London WC1A 1NU

A division of Scholastic Ltd
London - New York - Toronto - Sydney - Auckland
Mexico City - New Delhi - Hong Kong

Published in the UK by Scholastic Ltd, 2000.

ISBN 0 439 99947 2

10 9 8 7 6 5 4 3 2 1

Printed by Cox & Wyman Ltd, England

# Contents

1. Introduction                                    7
2. Bats: The Original Vampires                     13
3. Leeches: Bloodsucking Worms                     31
4. Bedbugs, Lice and Fleas:
   Nasty Insects                                   49
5. Sea Lampreys: Bloodsucking Fish                 63
6. Mosquitoes: The Ultimate Vampires              79

# INTRODUCTION

I don't know about you but I've never liked any variety of soup. It's not because I can't find any with ingredients I like – taste isn't the problem. I just find them boring to eat because it takes so long to spoon them into your mouth. Soups are food, but shouldn't food be solid or at least semi-solid? A liquid is something you *drink*. Because of my aversion I've always been intrigued by animal vampire creatures that never eat solid food and survive on what is certainly the most crimson of soups: blood! These creatures have a liquid diet for their whole lives!

Although blood appears to be red, it is actually

composed of a yellowish liquid called plasma and billions of cells. The vast majority of these cells are red and these red cells give blood its red colour. They look like doughnuts with holes that don't go all the way through. They're red because they contain a special protein called haemoglobin. This protein binds to the oxygen we inhale into our lungs when we breathe and transports it all over our body. It then picks up carbon dioxide for the return journey so we can exhale it from our lungs. Red cells are why blood is protein-packed and that's what animal vampires need to survive. To them we're just big bags of protein that leak nutritious blood when there is a hole in us!

Different groups of creatures are thirsty for blood for different reasons. Most of us have come across animals where only the female of the species has a blood lust: mosquitoes and other biting flies only need a protein boost before producing eggs, so if you're bitten by one, you know it's a she – the males are content with sipping nectar from flowers. With some other insects – bedbugs and body lice, for instance –

both sexes feed exclusively on blood. The same is true with vampire bats, sanguivorous leeches (sanguivorous is the technical term for blood-feeding – other species of leech swallow whole prey, flesh and all), and lampreys (although these fish may swallow some of the skin and innards of their victims too).

I've always wanted to make a film about these bloodsucking creatures and so I decided that the best way to do that was to let as many of them as possible take a blood meal from me on camera. Don't worry, I'm not mad! One of the special problems that faces animal vampires is having to take an involuntary blood donation from animals thousands of times their size or even more (we're a *million* times larger than a mosquito). To do it they have to approach stealthily and bite virtually painlessly. So I could be sure that letting myself be bitten wouldn't hurt too much. I also knew I wouldn't come to any harm. Most animal vampires only take insignificant quantities of blood – even a vampire bat only needs two tablespoons to drink its fill.

Blood-drinkers have another special problem

to overcome. When we're cut, fragments of another kind of cell, called platelets, gather at the site of the injury and stick to the edges of the wound. They release special chemicals that work in unison with other chemicals to start the process of blood-clotting so that the bleeding will stop. This process is why scabs form at the skin's surface. Animal vampires need to stop this from happening. If the blood that is flowing from their bite stops flowing, they won't get enough food. They overcome this problem by having chemicals called anti-coagulants in their saliva which stop the clotting process. These can be very efficient, as I found out when I was bitten by a leech. I bled for ten hours! And since the bite happened in the afternoon I had to have my legs bandaged so that when I went to bed I didn't soak the sheets in blood.

I must say, even though animal vampires are fascinating, there were times like the one I've just described when I felt slightly queasy and uncomfortable about being lunch for a leech or dinner for a bedbug. I suppose it's natural to feel revolted about being food for other animals.

Even so, I had great fun travelling around the world to meet the vampires and I really hope you enjoy reading about my adventures.

# Bats:
# The Original Vampires

The last few clods of earth thud onto the lid of the coffin until it's completely covered and the grave-digger turns to begin his next excavation. Suddenly there's a tremendous splintering sound, the grave-digger spins round to see a man who's meant to be dead, rising from the fresh grave. He looks hideous, clay is caked in his hair, his fingers are bleeding from where he's scrabbled at the coffin lid and blood trickles from his lips where he's injured himself in the struggle to escape from his premature burial. The grave-digger screams and runs – surely this creature is a bloodsucking ghost!

This story could have been told in many cultures for thousands of years. Since ancient times blood has been a symbol of life – only the living have blood that flows. Supernatural creatures give themselves life by drinking it. In fact, what the grave-digger saw doesn't need a supernatural explanation. Catalepsy is a real medical condition, a form of suspended animation where people can see and hear but not move. If these people are buried alive and the catalepsy ends, they might break out from the soil and set off a legend about a bloodsucking ghost.

Nowadays, if you mention vampires people always think of bats. As a naturalist I've always wondered why. Real blood-feeding species are only found in the tropical Americas and it wasn't until 1526 that an explorer first reported their existence. But there have been myths about bloodsucking humans in Europe and the Middle East for thousands of years, since long before blood-feeding bats were ever known about. The bats were named after the monsters in European legends. The link between 'human' vampires and the flying mammals was reinforced by the author, Bram Stoker, who in 1897 became intrigued by blood-feeding bats, and wrote his famous book *Dracula*. In this novel the bloodsucking Count Dracula can shift his shape into anything he wants to, including a bat. From that point on, bats and bloodsucking monsters would always be connected in our imaginations.

There are actually three species of vampire bat: the white-winged, hairy-legged, and common vampire. The first two actually *look* very cute, with big bulbous eyes and long hair, but they're rare and little is known about them (except that they attack sleeping birds and feed on their blood – not so cute, I must admit). The common vampire is the species that has been intensively studied, mainly because it feeds on the blood of mammals, including us and our livestock, and it can transmit rabies when it bites.

From what I'd read about real vampire bats,

they seemed just as intriguing as their supernatural namesakes. They can move like no other bat and even look after each other if one is sick. I couldn't wait to meet them. For my first encounter I travelled to Southern Mexico. The home of vampires has changed a lot since they were first discovered. Much impenetrable jungle has been cleared for farms, but pockets still remain. With our Mexican guide and four mules to carry our heavy filming equipment, the cameraman and I trekked to a patch of rainforest that hid the entrance to a mysterious bat cave.

The cave was quite well lit and spacious – we didn't have to wriggle through holes or anything to get into it. We had to wear masks over our noses and mouths, though. This was because we were walking on top of mounds of bat guano (droppings) which is made up of the remains of fruit and insects that some of the bats couldn't digest. There was a chance that this manure could be covered in a fungus and if we inhaled the spores from it we'd be risking a dangerous lung disease. Of course the guano was from other species of bat, not the vampires we were interested in, who feed *exclusively* on blood. We saw and smelt the remains of *their* meals beneath a deep fissure in the cave wall. The rock was covered in a dark red, almost black slime – undigested blood! The slick produced a strong smell of ammonia. Somewhere in the dark recesses of the cleft there must be a colony of vampire bats. We set up our filming lights and waited for dusk.

Looking out of the cave entrance I could see it was getting dark. Bats began to move en masse to begin their nocturnal wanderings. Thousands of them swirled and chattered around our heads. Their flying ability was phenomenal and even though we could feel the breeze from their wings they never tangled in our hair. It was very exciting. We ran the camera in slow motion as the bats continued to drop out of the fissure and hoped that we would catch the bats' incredible speed and manoeuvrability on film.

Back home in Bristol at the production studio, we waited with baited breath to see the results of our work. But as we looked at the screen, we couldn't make out one kind of bat from another, even in slow motion they flew too fast. There was no way we could tell whether we'd been filming vampires or not. This was disappointing, and meant I had to find another way to get up close and personal with vampire bats.

I found out about a scientist, Dr Uwe Schmidt, in Bonn, Germany, who has kept his own colony of vampire bats for twenty years or so. He was willing to help us film some close-up details of behaviour and, most importantly, let me hold and perhaps even be bitten by one of his vampires!

Filming captive animals is sometimes the only way that aspects of behaviour can be recorded, particularly if the animals concerned are easily disturbed, spend much of their time in hiding or are small or nocturnal or all of these things. But that doesn't mean that filming under captive conditions is easy. There has to be meticulous preparation, the animals have to be relaxed so they behave naturally, and it has to be remembered that their welfare is paramount. For the vampire-filming in Bonn, colonies of bats had to be moved from the wire cages where they normally live into specially constructed filming sets, but they needed ten days to feel totally at ease in them. Even the simplest of acts – feeding – wasn't going to be simple. These vampires have lost many of their wild instincts and are used to drinking their blood meals from a bottle. They would have to be trained to bite and lap up blood as they do in the wild. But I was determined to improve on those flight shots of unidentifiable bats we'd filmed in Mexico with some really dramatic footage. We planned to construct a special escape-proof flight-tunnel so that if we were lucky we might be able to track our camera right alongside a vampire in flight.

Before all that, the first thing I did when I arrived at Bonn University was to meet the vampire bats. Dr Schmidt slowly opened the door of the set so that I could peek inside. The bats – about sixteen of them – were hanging upside down from some rough wooden beams. They looked relaxed and it seemed they had acclimatized to the set. They were also smaller than I had expected, with tailless bodies some nine centimetres long. When one unfurled its wings I could see they had a span of forty centimetres or so. Their fur was greyish brown, a bit lighter on their tummies. One looked at me and I stared back into its beady, black eyes. It wrinkled its compact muzzle, which seemed swollen – but then I noticed that all the bats had a bulbous snout, so it wasn't unusual. The specialist tools for feeding on blood are hidden in the muzzle. We'll find out about those later.

Another bat had its back to me but then it swivelled round, revealing a tiny baby clinging to its chest. Dr Schmidt said this was a thriving captive colony and there were up to ten births a year. A single baby was the norm, but there were sometimes twins. The bats could mate at any time of year and gave birth after a seven-month pregnancy. For the first month the helpless babies live on their mother's milk. (In the wild, she has to fly with babies on board when she wants to feed.) The babies grow fast in the second month and the diet of milk is supplemented with regurgitated blood. By the fourth month they can accompany their mother, flying under their own steam, when she's looking for prey.

We filmed the family life of this colony for the next three days. One of the bats, a young female, was off-colour and didn't move to the feeding bottle. She would have starved to death in about three days but, remarkably, the other bats looked after her. They groomed her fur and then transferred blood from their last meal into her mouth. This was touching indeed – friendship amongst vampires! But there are rules: the female must have helped her roost-mates in the past because if a bat refuses to feed other colony members it is shunned and won't be helped by them.

Now we had to film a vampire actually feeding. One bat had been trained to bite through a piece of cow-hide, but I really wanted to experience being bitten myself. We hoped he would oblige! (Dr Schmidt's colony is, of course, rabies free, so I wasn't putting myself at risk.)

The cameras rolled as I gently lifted the reluctant diner on to my arm. He sat still and I moved his head close to my skin. Vampires have heat-sensors in their snouts to locate veins close to the surface. He didn't find one to his liking and crept delicately on all fours along my arm. Vampires have strong limbs and modified thumbs for walking, running and hopping. In the wild, being light on his feet would help him avoid detection. If he was scuttling over animals much larger than himself to find a bite-site, and he was noticed, he would have to take evasive action to avoid being injured by swishing tails or kicking hooves. Bats have the ability to jump in virtually any direction.

My vampire didn't have to worry about being swatted by me, I didn't want to do anything that could disturb him from biting, but sadly his wild instincts had been lost. Because he'd spent his life drinking blood from the bottle he just didn't know what to do!

So we didn't manage to film an actual bite but we could still film the animal *drinking*. By using a pipette we dropped blood on to my arm. It was amazing to watch: the bat didn't suck the blood up, it lapped it up as if it was a dog drinking water from a bowl. There are grooves in its tongue which expand and contract and the pumping action has the effect of drawing the liquid into channels in its lower lip and into the mouth. A vampire needs about two tablespoons of blood a day. That means that in a year a colony of 100 drinks an amount equivalent to the blood in twenty-five cows.

We'd filmed family life and feeding and now we wanted to capture the flight of the vampire on celluloid. A take-off was first on our list. When a bat was on the ground, we ran the camera and clapped – giving it a fright initiated a take-off. Vampires are the only bats that can take off vertically. They leap straight into the air before swooping away, just like Harrier jump-jets.

Now we had to use our flight tunnel to film the bats when they were airborne. It was the university holidays so we set this up in a lecture theatre. The bat-proof tunnel was more than four metres long and made of black netting, with a window of clear perspex all along it. Two bat boxes were suspended at either end and once the bats stopped 'hanging around' in their boxes and got the hang of flying they'd do lengths of the tunnel, twisting and turning at the end of each length, like Olympic swimmers doing a tumble-turn in a pool. Our camera was outside the tunnel pressed against the perspex window. It was on a dolly – a camera platform with wheels – and this whole contraption rested on a set of rails. As a bat took off, the cameraman ran as fast as he could, pushing the camera and dolly ahead of him. About once every twenty goes, the vampire would fly level with the camera and the cameraman would keep up. It was thrilling to see the developed film, the slowed-down pictures make you really feel as if you're flying right alongside a vampire bat.

In the wild, vampires used to cause little harm but because of the deforestation I saw in Mexico (which is happening throughout South America too) nature is out of kilter; we've upset the natural balance. The bats once preyed on wild rainforest mammals but since so much of the rainforest has been cut down, these are much rarer now and their place has been taken by our domestic livestock. Cows and horses are abundant and a much easier prey, so the populations of vampire bats are at an all-time high. Their attacks wouldn't be *too* harmful if they didn't transmit the virus that causes paralytic rabies. This virus is carried in their saliva and is transmitted when they bite.

Because there are serious outbreaks leading to many livestock deaths, vampire bats are being controlled. The problem is that the people who kill the bats can be indiscriminate, killing other kinds of bats as well as vampires. Short-tailed fruit bats are declining and that's a problem because they can disperse up to 60,000 seeds in a night (in their droppings), so without them the rainforests will never recover. Insectivorous bats (i.e. bats that eat insects) have also been killed. These are useful too because they keep down the mosquitoe population that transmits yellow fever and malaria, human diseases which can be fatal.

Now that this destruction of other species of bats has been noticed in tropical America, the vampire hunters are being much more careful. They trap bats in nets and release the harmless species. The captured vampires are daubed with a poison. As I saw in Germany, grooming between members of the colony is frequent, so when the bats return carrying the deadly load other bats lick the fur, swallow some of the poison and die too. Whole colonies can be destroyed in this way.

Hopefully this battle won't spread to more remote regions. Vampires don't deserve to be hunted to extinction. Unlike Count Dracula, they don't show any intentional malice towards us. By clearing the land for our livestock, we simply gave them an opportunity which they took. In fact, in the long run, they may even be helpful to us. The anti-clotting agent in their saliva is already being tested to help victims of heart attacks and strokes.

I'd seen the bats in the laboratory now, but I was still desperate to meet them in the wild. So I went back to Mexico and visited a ranch where they are still quite common. I sat quietly in the corner of a stable, watching the one long narrow window intently. The horse quickly got used to me and soon lay down to sleep. By 2 am I could hardly keep my eyes open, but then I heard a gentle fluttering outside the window. My eyes opened wide and, with a curved manoeuvre of superb precision, a bat came straight through the window. But was it a vampire?

I soon knew when it landed on the ground, scuttling about on all fours. Only a vampire would do that. It cautiously approached the horse and quickly clambered on to its back. The captive animal in Germany had forgotten how to bite, but this one certainly hadn't and bit almost instantly. The horse didn't even flinch as the large, razor-sharp teeth made a painless three millimetre incision. The anti-coagulant in a vampire's saliva is called draculin and it's twenty times stronger than any other anti-clotting agent. There's another ingredient in the saliva to keep red blood cells from sticking together and yet another stops the constriction of blood-vessels which take blood to the wound. This chemical cocktail meant the horse bled freely, so the bat could lap up a good meal.

After a while, my first wild vampire finished its dinner and took a few steps forward before launching itself away from the horse. With a clever twist of its leathery wings, it was through the window and away into the sub-tropical night.

★ ★ ★ ★ ★

I've gained many insights into the lives of vampire bats, and I must say I really admire them. They're a fantastic example of how the evolutionary process works to make animals specialized for a particular way of life. Feeding on nothing else but blood, the bats must use cunning to get close to their prey. They approach in an unexpected and 'unbatlike' way – walking, running and jumping. Once there, they use their fangs to bite painlessly with surgical precision, injecting a saliva with remarkable properties to keep blood flowing from the wound.

There's no doubt these bloodsuckers have a bad reputation, but there's much we can learn from them – and after all, like you and me, they need food to survive!

# Vampires – Fact Box

● Vampire bats don't suck blood, they lap it.

● After a seven-month pregnancy, a vampire bat has a single baby, perhaps two. For the first month the young feed on blood, in the second they feed on blood regurgitated by their mother.

● Vampire bats can live for thirty years in captivity and for about twelve years in the wild.

● They can only survive in the tropics because blood doesn't have enough energy to sustain bats if they have to use energy to keep warm as well.

● Vampire bats have the fewest teeth of any bat because they don't have to chew their food.

# Leeches:
# Bloodsucking worms

The hairy legs of the swamp creature pushed through the black ooze and its head, with two bulging eyes, soon followed. Folded beneath the head there is a strange apparatus for feeding. If prey came within range, this weaponry – which has spines at its tip – would shoot out and impale it. Another creature – this time a vegetarian – moved out from the mud. Rocks stuck together to form a tube enveloped its body, and gave protection from the predators. A fish flipped into view. It was armed with three sharp spines along its back and had a blood-red throat as if it had been slit.

I moved more weed and mud aside to see if there was anything else in the bottom of the net. The swamp creature was a dragonfly larva about the size of my thumbnail, it wouldn't menace anything larger than a tadpole. Later in the summer it would leave the pond, and crawl up a stem to transform into a gauzy-winged adult. The vegetarian encased in stone was another insect about the same size: eventually this caddis larva would also leave the pond taking wing as an adult caddis fly. The fish, a tiddler, was a three-spined stickle-back. In spring the males have a bright red throat which they show off during courtship.

Something else moved just to the side of the stickleback. Jet black, its slimy body shone in the sun. I could see it was made up of segments, like an earthworm. In fact, it was about the size of your average earthworm, and as it slithered out from the weeds I could see there was a circular disc at its back end. Excitedly I pulled it from the net and cupped it in my hands. The disc was a sucker that attached to my skin, and there was another smaller sucker at the front. With these the leech could hang on even if I turned my hand upside-down or even shook it. I was ten and this was the first leech I'd ever seen.

I took the creature home and watched it in an aquarium. I hoped to see it drink the stickleback's blood and I even put my hand under the water to see if it would latch on to me. I thought all leeches were bloodsuckers, but this one only ate blood if it was wrapped up in flesh and could be swallowed whole. The leech attacked and consumed a pond snail first. I watched, incredulous, as the mollusc disappeared and the lump passed down the leech's body just like a snake swallowing a rabbit. Worms were the leech's favourite prey, even when they were as long as its own body. The food would be grabbed with the powerful sucker and then the leech would open its mouth at one end of the worm – it didn't seem to matter from which end it started. Slowly but surely the leech would work its jaws along the worm's body, swallowing each pink segment one after the other. At the end of this process the leech was so fat and swollen it could hardly move. I let my pet go after a week or two and had nothing much to do with leeches until much later, when I became the prey for some bloodsucking leeches that tracked me down on land.

Tasmania is a large island off the southern coast of Australia. Hot in summer but quite cool in winter – Antarctica isn't that far away – it's a paradise for naturalists. Foxes haven't managed to cross the sea from the mainland where they were introduced by people and have decimated much of Australia's original wildlife. The creatures there weren't used to being hunted by foxes and hadn't evolved any defences so they were – and are – easy prey. Many species have become rare and some are extinct.

I could see it was different on Tasmania as we left Hobart, the capital city, and headed for a small island just off the coast. We crossed on a ferry to Bruny Island and it was dusk as we headed for our cottage. There were so many animals on the road that we had to drive really carefully. They were all native Australian marsupials (mammals that have pouches for holding their babies). Long-nosed bandicoots scurried in front of the car and we saw two quolls, or native Australian cats. On the mainland these are extinct. Tasmania and its islands are the only place where you can see these beautiful creatures which have grey fur with big white spots. There were wallabies too. If our headlights shone at just the right angle, we could see their eyes glowing in the dark as their owners bounded across the road.

There was obviously plenty of food for the leeches we'd come to see. Given the chance they would suck the blood of any mammal. But I knew the leeches wouldn't be just anywhere. They can't stand drying out, so we needed to find a particular kind of habitat where leeches literally drip from the leaves.

The next morning we reached our destination. I felt like I'd gone back to the time of the dinosaurs. We were surrounded by the kinds of plants that were around then: tree-ferns – great clusters of leathery, feathery leaves held aloft by fibrous black trunks. Eerie shrieks came from somewhere in the forest. I imagined they were pterodactyls but the cries came from a party of black cockatoos. Everything was sopping wet and we squelched through carpets of moss and a thick layer of sodden humus: we were in land leech heaven.

There was no need to go looking for them – they would surely find me. Meals can be few and far between, and although they can survive for up to a year without food, they have to make the most of any opportunity. The vibrations from my footsteps would alert them first and they would then make their way towards the disturbance.

I spotted the first one when it was three metres away. Its greenish-black body had stripes of sulphur-yellow. It moved in a way that is unique to leeches. The hind sucker attached to a leaf while the head end stretched forwards. When the front sucker was attached, the rear one was released and the rest of the body was drawn forwards too. Then the process began again. No other animals have exploited the sucker mode of locomotion as successfully as leeches have.

Between each move the leech stretched upwards, sinuously waving its thin head like a snake. It was sensing me. Chemical receptors could smell me and detect the carbon dioxide from my breath. Out of the corner of my eye I saw something move. Another leech was only thirty centimetres away! Dangling from the tip of a tree-fern frond, it stretched hungrily towards me. To get it even more excited I breathed on it. The leech gently balanced on its rear sucker and swayed, probing the air like a blind man tapping his cane. This close, the leech could probably make out my shape. Along its body there are receptors that detect changes in light intensity so when I shifted position the patterns of light and dark would change.

I looked down and realized I was surrounded. Leeches were approaching from all sides. Two were climbing from my sandals on to my toes and another three were searching for a feeding site on my shin. I let this trio on my leg be, and asked the soundman if he'd mind gathering up the other leeches and taking them back into the bush – three leeches feeding on me was quite enough! Then I was filmed as the leeches took their meal. At first I felt a tickling sensation – the bloodsuckers were gently rocking their heads using their toothed jaws like miniature saws to make an incision into my skin. The leeches were as thin as shoe-laces but that would change as they gorged on my blood.

I didn't feel a thing once they were through my skin, because they'd injected a cocktail of chemicals including pain killers. This cocktail also contains a special substance – unique to leeches – called hirudin. Like draculin in bats, hirudin stops blood clotting. Normally if I cut myself there's a scab in five minutes. If that happened when the leech was feeding, it couldn't carry on sucking, so hirudin helps keep the blood flowing freely.

It was a peculiar feeling watching other creatures feasting on me, especially when I could actually see them swelling up. The leeches expanded to about nine times their original size. According to the text books, a feeding bout lasts about forty minutes and then the bloated leech drops off; but my leeches were still firmly attached an hour after they'd started sucking my blood. I decided they must have had enough and flicked them off. Now they certainly weren't stringy, having the appearance of fat slugs. Slowly they crawled under logs or into the leaf litter to hide and digest their meal.

My leg was covered in blood and, as it was mid-afternoon, I hoped the bleeding would stop by bedtime or the owners of the bed-and-breakfast where we were staying would think I'd murdered someone in my bed. But seven hours later my bites were still bleeding and I had to bandage my leg to stop the sheets turning crimson. Leech hirudin is amazing stuff. This time it was inconvenient for me, but one day it might help me as it has helped so many others unlucky enough to have had a certain type of serious injury that the bites of leeches can help to heal.

There's a picture on an ancient Egyptian tomb

of leeches being used to treat someone. In fact they have been used medicinally for thousands of years to treat every ailment from headaches to possession by demons! In the 1800s doctors in Paris used to treat patients with thirty or more leeches at a time and in 1863 Paris hospitals used six million leeches! (Another seven million were used in London.) The species used by physicians lives in water. It's a handsome creature, black in colour with an exquisite pattern of orange and yellow. It was such a popular animal that gentlewomen in French society sometimes had dresses designed which copied the patterns on leeches' bodies! Unfortunately, collecting specimens when 'leech mania' was at its height made the medicinal leech an endangered species. It's still rare and protected in Europe today. Even when over-collecting stopped, it couldn't recover its numbers because of the number of ponds that had been drained or polluted.

Nowadays the leeches used in medicine are bred specially for the purpose. Of course doctors now know leeches can't cure coughs, tumours, headaches and mental illness, but they can be crucial in re-attachment surgery. People who have lost fingers, toes and even ears and noses in accidents can have them grafted back on with the help of leeches. Tiny blood-vessels take time to grow in these grafts and, until they do, the application of leeches gives the blood a way out and creates an artificial flow of blood through the grafted tissues.

Medicinal leeches and the land leeches that fed from me aren't fussy about the type of blood they drink: humans, horses, frogs and birds could all provide a meal. But there's one leech species that, as far as we know, only drinks one type of blood. This extraordinary vampire is *only* found in tropical Africa and only where there are hippos.

Finding these leeches by getting close to their prey would certainly be a challenge. Even though they're vegetarian, hippos are among the most dangerous animals on earth. At three tons they weigh as much as three Land Rovers and have a mouth that's sixty centimetres across with tusks inside that are fifty centimetres long. If you get between them and water – or anywhere near a baby when the parents are close by – they may charge at you and you can be trampled or bitten. The sheer size of this mammal makes that a pretty frightening proposition.

Also, in many parts of Africa, hippos spend most of the day in water, only coming out at night to feed. So to see whether they have leeches on their bodies, you'd have to be able to see underwater or in darkness.

Our research showed, however, that there was one place where hippos spend most of the day on the land. That place was near the town of Garoua in the Cameroon. There we would find a very special hippo that would allow me to approach closely, even take me for a ride!

The film crew and I went to a game camp on the river where the hippos lived. The trackers left at sunrise the day after we arrived to locate the place where the herd was spending the day. They returned later in the morning with news of the hippos' whereabouts, so we stowed all our gear in a wooden boat and set off downstream. On our way our guides told me about the tunnels in the riverside vegetation which hippos use to get to and from shady clearings where they doze during the day.

Shortly after we arrived, I was thrilled to find myself in a hippo tunnel for the first time. My senses were so alert, I felt I could have heard a pin drop from ten metres away – even though a dropped pin wouldn't make a sound in this terrain! We were squelching through deep hippo footprints in thick mud. The low tunnels about one and a half metres high, the height of a hippo's back, arched over our heads. We had to stoop as we walked and be completely silent. A light breeze blew in our faces and every now and then the trackers checked its direction by using the flame of a lighter. (The flame would, of course, lean over in the direction the wind was blowing.) We had to stay downwind of the hippos. If they caught our scent they'd flee into dense vegetation or even stampede down the tunnels towards us. If that happened, the hippos wouldn't stop and we'd have to jump very rapidly sideways to avoid being trampled.

After wending our way through the swampy tunnels for an hour, the lead tracker motioned for us to stop. I heard branches breaking ahead of us. The cameraman followed as I crawled slowly forwards. There, a little way ahead, was an eye! The hippo's body was obscured by vegetation, but I could see patches of pinkish skin through the leaves. I turned to whisper to the cameraman as the huge creature lumbered across the path in front of us. In the sunlight I could see red droplets glistening on its body.

Centuries ago the ancient Greeks thought hippos sweated blood, but the sticky pink oil they produce is a moisturizer and sunscreen to protect their delicate skin. I scanned its body with my binoculars and the cameraman did the same with his powerful telephoto lens, but we couldn't find any leeches hanging from its hide. Then the creature sensed something was near and my heart stopped as it lifted its head and looked straight at us. Hippos have poor eyesight so it could only have discerned some odd shapes different from the background of leaves and twigs. Would it charge? My whole body tensed as I prepared to leap out of the tunnel into the bushes at the side. Then, with a snort, the hippo turned and walked – it didn't even run – in the opposite direction.

Now we needed to inspect a hippo closely for leeches. To do that we travelled back to Garoua where we met a very special hippo indeed. Her name was Africa and she was found orphaned when she was just five months old. An African called Sabou fed her with maize and sweet potato and they developed a special friendship. The river where she lives runs right through the town and sometimes she even walks along a busy road, holding up the traffic, to find Sabou in the local cinema where he works, because she likes being with him. As long as he was around she'd let me lay in the shallow water with her and perhaps even let me clamber on her back. I hoped she'd also let me feel for leeches in the folds of skin around the base of her legs. However, just before we arrived, a problem had developed. Africa, now seven, had a mate, and in the water this male hippo guarded her jealously. Even when she was on land, if she was away too long he'd grunt and bellow until she slipped back into the river with him.

His presence meant that our filming took three days rather than one since we could only film when he was far enough away for me and the camera crew to have enough warning if and when he decided to attack. We didn't fancy being chomped by a jealous boyfriend that had ivory teeth more than fifty centimetres long!

When the male's back was turned, I ran my hands along Africa's hide. Her skin was amazing – smooth like a baby's. Latched on near her tail I found what I was looking for – a hippopotamus leech! It was reddish brown in colour, presumably for camouflage on the hippo's hide. That would protect it from being too obvious to the oxpecker birds that pick off parasites from the skin of large animals. Rather than using suckers to move, it wriggled like an earthworm. Keeping its body flat against the hippo's body prevents it from being dislodged by strong river currents or the swimming movement of its host. I clenched my hand around it as tightly as I could, but the leech still slipped out through my fingers. In fact this unique leech is very much used to getting in and out of tight spaces: scientists now believe this species of leech only breeds when it is actually inside the rectum of a hippo!

When the time comes, mature adult leeches crawl under the hippo's tail and force their way inside the hippo's bottom to mate. Nice and cosy! We still don't know how the leeches cope with the hostile environment that is a hippo's bottom. It's difficult to imagine what it must be like in there, but it is certainly highly acidic with very low levels of oxygen.

This extraordinary story was only discovered in 1994. In the natural world there are many more such stories just waiting to be told. That's why I'm passionate about making wildlife films: we can show the amazing discoveries made by scientists to millions of people. Whenever you research a science programme there's always something that's utterly surprising. Certainly, I'd never have believed that one of the highlights of a programme on animal vampires would be a leech that spent time in a hippo's bum!

# Leeches – Fact Box

- There are 650 known species of leeches.
- The largest leech discovered measured forty-five centimetres.
- The leech has thirty-two brains – thirty-one more than a human.
- The Hirudo leech has three jaws with 100 teeth on each jaw – making 300 teeth in all.
- Wales was once one of the major leech collecting areas of Europe.

Me with a vampire bat.

Great vampire bat feeds on pig blood.

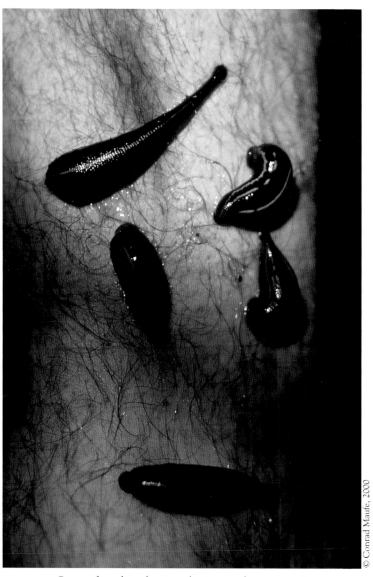

Some leeches begin their meal – on me!

The meal is over.

This hippo is an unknowing leech carrier.

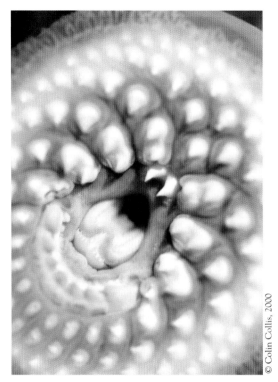

The lamprey's mouth in close-up.

This one's stuck to my head . . .

. . . and this lamprey came swimming with me.

© Alastair MacEwen/www.osf.uk.com, 2000

A common cat flea.

© Tina Carvalho/www.osf.uk.com, 2000

The same type of flea under a microscope.

© John Forsdyke/www.osf.uk.com, 2000

The head louse – the 'claws' keep them clinging on.

© Images Colour Library, 2000

This mosquito has just taken its fill of blood.

A mosquito – one of nature's greatest killers in close-up.

# Bedbugs, Lice and Fleas: Nasty Insects

The great bed was warm and comfortable. The portraits above the fireplace glowed orange from the dying embers in the hearth: their subjects – the eighteenth-century owners of the castle in which I was now attempting to sleep – seemed to be watching me. A storm raged outside and every now and then the room was fully illuminated with a blinding white lightning flash. I knew it was going to be hard to sleep: after all, this bedroom was full of vampires, all thirsty for my blood!

Through my half-closed eyes I could see the creatures leaving their hiding-places: cracks and crevices under peeling wallpaper; the tiny gap behind an oak wardrobe pushed tight against the wall; even the holes in the frames of the portraits. I wondered if the subjects had guessed that, hundreds of years after sitting for the artist, every night their painted faces would be covered in crawling mahogany-coloured creatures looking like mobile brown lentils. This room had a heavy infestation of bedbugs, and as I drifted into unconsciousness, the sickly-sweet smell of the oily secretion that the vampires produce was overpowering.

These bloodsuckers have been with us humans from Stone Age times, since we first set up semi-permanent camps in caves. By sticking closely to us – often literally – these parasites have spread around the world. Nowadays their lives are so interwoven with ours they can't do without us. When our relationship started it was a golden age for the ancestors of bedbugs. They had blood on tap twenty-four hours a day. That's because many of the caves that early humans inhabited also had colonies of bats. The bloodsucking bugs fed on the winged mammals in the ceiling by day and then came down to ground level at night to prey on the early humans as they slept.

The descendants of those cave-dwelling vampires scuttled towards me now, attracted by my breath and the warmth of my body. So desperate were they to reach me that some even dropped from the ceiling. Once on the bedclothes they clambered towards the exposed flesh of my arms. Once there, these oval insects – a little more than five millimetres long – delicately put their legs on my skin, waving their antennae over me to make a final check on their meal before biting. Their sharp mouth parts probed beneath my skin to find a vein which they could tap into. They looked flat at first, but they soon swelled with my blood. Their segmented bodies have special flexible membranes to allow for this expansion during a meal. As with other vampires, it's important that their meal flows freely so bedbugs have an anti-coagulant in their blood. Some of the bedbugs were miniature replicas of the larger ones: these young ones are called nymphs, and they moult their skins five times before becoming adults.

Each bug fed for ten minutes or so. The adult females would use the protein they'd extracted from my veins to produce eggs. If they can get two blood meals a week they can lay six or seven eggs in that time. White and oblong, about a millimetre long, these eggs are laid where the bedbugs hide by day. Remarkably, one bedbug is recorded as having survived for 550 days without a meal.

Wherever the bedbug mouthparts had penetrated, my skin came up in a small red bump but that was the only clue that I'd been a meal for them. There'd be no side-effects either; bedbugs have never been proved guilty of transmitting diseases to humans, but the same can't be said about the loathsome creatures feeding on my other arm: body lice!

These insects evolved from head lice, to whom they are closely related. Body lice are ten to twenty per cent larger but other than that they're difficult to tell apart. Migrating from the head to the body when humans started wearing clothes, body lice now live their entire lives between our skin and clothing, or sometimes between skin and bedding. They clambered around the hairs of my arm like monkeys in a jungle. Each of their six legs has a single claw at the end worked by a powerful muscle. A hair shaft fits perfectly between the curved claw and the leg, like pliers fitting around a tube or pipe. That's why they are difficult to scratch off. Their grip is extremely tight and their bodies are very flat so they can cling close and weather a storm of even the most severe scratching. Now about a dozen of these tiny vampires had their legs hooked around my hairs. Suddenly, tube-like mouthparts armed with minute teeth and spikes for piercing skin protruded from their heads and embedded themselves in my flesh. Then the grey bodies reddened with my blood. Once attached, the mouthparts continue sucking even if the bodies are cut away, and their bite is so powerful they can withstand a load of four kilograms before losing their grip.

Well-fed female body lice can lay between 200 and 300 eggs. These 'nits' are glued on to hair or into the seams and hems of clothing. In ten days or so, incubated by the warmth of their host's body, the larva swallows the remaining liquid inside the egg and large amounts of air. By doing this it rapidly expands, flipping open the egg cap to hatch and begin searching for its first blood meal, which – unless the clothes have been discarded – isn't far away.

Head and body lice are dangerous because they can transmit the typhus virus in their saliva and excrement, or if their bodies are crushed and rubbed into broken flesh. It's probable that the defeat of Napoleon's armies in Russia in 1812 was due to this disease. I wasn't at risk because the body lice on my arm were bred under sterile conditions in a research laboratory. The bedroom with the portraits and old fireplace was, in fact, a film set and I'd insisted the crew and researchers knew where every bedbug and louse was at all times. Even for a naturalist like me these bloodsuckers are revolting and I didn't want them escaping and turning up unexpectedly. The cracks and crevices from which the bedbugs had emerged had been made so we could film them creeping from a hiding place.

Luckily, in this day and age, very few of us will have direct contact with body lice and bedbugs. Washing our bodies and clothes and keeping our houses clean keeps them at bay. My ordeal for the filming was the only time I'd ever been attacked by them. That's because they mainly prey on people that are destitute because of war or natural disasters, such as cyclones or earthquakes. In disaster zones, living conditions are crowded, personal hygiene is neglected and people huddle together for warmth, often sleeping in their clothes: perfect conditions for bloodsucking parasites, which can reach plague proportions.

Head lice don't need unhygienic conditions, of course. They thrive in clean hair and in the warmth of our centrally-heated buildings. Every year about fourteen million children get them in the United States alone. The trouble is they are becoming resistant to many common pesticides so parents have to use special fine-toothed combs to remove them by hand.

Many of us will have had direct contact with

head lice some time in our lives, and if we have pet dogs or cats another set of bloodsuckers will probably have featured in our lives too. To meet these creatures I was filmed entering an abandoned room that had been lived in by a cat. The pet and its owners had moved house six months before but they'd left thousands of vampires behind. The cat fleas had been waiting for a new warm-blooded mammal to enter their resting place – that mammal was me. The cameras rolled as I walked into the room. Once the vibrations from my footsteps were transmitted through the floor the carpet began to move. It was as if the dust itself was coming to life. I'd taken off my shoes and socks and rolled up my trousers, so we could watch the parasites attack.

I put my flashlight down and it illuminated an area of carpet. It seethed with a layer of shiny brown fleas. A few leapt towards me, then hundreds, soaring through the air in a leap many times their own length. (Cat fleas can easily jump over thirty centimetres). Hungry fleas have been known to jump 600 times an hour for three days trying to find a host. Moving black spots covered my feet and ankles but they weren't moving for long. They stopped to bite and it felt as if hundreds of microscopic pins were piercing my skin. Inside their heads, fleas have a ball of resilin, which is nature's most effective elastic – ninety-seven per cent efficient. This is next to a hammer-like bar which is connected to the piercing mouthparts. By tilting its head, the flea distorts the elastic ball which then springs back into shape, driving the mouthparts into the skin.

We filmed some of the fleas under the microscope and watching that footage was the first time I'd had a really good look at them. Lice are flattened from back to front but fleas are flattened from side to side. Seen from the front it looks as if they are standing on edge. That's so they can 'swim' along the hairs of their host, propelling themselves with their long slender legs and pushing through with their heads, which are shaped like the keel of a boat. At high magnification, I was astounded at the combs and bristles covering the fleas' legs and bodies. These allow the fleas to anchor themselves in hair if they need to and also provide protection for their delicate joints.

We couldn't tell the sex of the fleas but I knew any females would put the protein from my blood to good use. They'd manufacture eggs which, when laid would drop from the host. Bedbugs and lice have an incomplete metamorphosis – the young animals (nymphs) are pretty similar to the adults. But fleas are like butterflies, having a complete metamorphosis with a larva that's totally different from the adult and a transformation or pupal stage inside a cocoon. Larval fleas are legless, maggot-like creatures that don't suck blood. Instead they feed on skin flakes and other debris. Once fully grown they change into pupae. Inside these pupae the adult 'vampire' fleas are formed. If there are no mammals nearby to jump aboard, the fleas will wait – sometimes for months, as these fleas had waited for me.

So we'd filmed the biology of fleas but I still had to get them off me. I put the clothes I'd had on straight into a freezer so any remaining parasites would freeze to death. Next I filled a huge bath with water, deep enough to submerge myself completely. I held my nose and ducked under the surface. Holding my breath I opened my eyes. The surface of the water swarmed with swimming fleas (they can't survive under water). The crew used a net to collect the insects and when I left the bath I was free of them. The aftermath of my flea attack just left me with red raised bumps on my ankles and between my toes as well, a terrible itching sensation that lasted for two or three days. Flea bites can, however, be much more serious than that.

Fleas usually specialize in bloodsucking from single species – that's why cat fleas are given that name. But if fleas are hungry, any animal will do – including humans. Transferring from one type of host to another is when fleas can become really dangerous. The plague or Black Death is primarily a disease of rats – rat fleas transmit a bacterium when they bite which causes the illness. But if rats start dying off, their fleas bite us. Throughout history the Black Death has been a virulent and dramatic disease. In fourteenth century Italy some cities lost every second citizen to the plague, and throughout Europe at least a quarter of the population died from it. Another epidemic, London's Great Plague of 1665, led to the deaths of 70,000 people out of a population of 460,000. Even now plague is still with us, breaking out periodically in the USSR, South East Asia and even the USA.

# Nasty Insects – Fact Box

• Bloodsucking insects rarely kill animals directly but 16,000 cows and horses were killed by blackfly in Romania in 1923.

• A parasite is an animal that obtains its nutrition at the expense of another organism. It doesn't usually kill its host.

• The earliest evidence of louse infection comes from Egyptian tombs where lice and their eggs were found mummified with their hosts.

• If a house is left vacant and it has a bedbug population, they'll migrate to neighbouring houses along gas, electricity and water pipe lines.

# Sea Lampreys:
# Bloodsucking Fish

This vampire lies hidden amongst rocks in the cool water. Right on the top of its head there is a hole, a single nostril. It has a well-developed sense of smell which it uses for finding the way to its breeding grounds. Perhaps it even locates concentrations of the prey on whose blood it feeds by their odour. Red-veined eyes bulge from the sides of its head and with these it scans the water above for any moving shape. The creature is very deep in the water and even though it's a sunny day only a small amount of light penetrates from the surface – but there is just enough for it to see.

Suddenly a silhouette appears and a streamlined vampire attacks. Flexing its sinuous body it glides vertically up through the water. The predator has a system of electro-receptors on its head and close up it can detect the electrical impulses generated by the heart and muscles of its prey. This simple picture of the body electricity of its victim guides the final attack. To reduce water-resistance while swimming into position, the vampire keeps its mouth closed; but just before striking the mouth flares open, revealing a circular suction cup with rings of sharp teeth. It slams the sucker into the side of its victim and latches on. The prey thrashes violently to dislodge the attacker, but to no avail – the vampire's grip is just too powerful.

A bloodsucking sea lamprey is now attached to the side of a lake trout. These fish are fifty-nine metres below the surface of Lake Huron, one of North America's five Great Lakes. Lampreys are primitive fish that have been around for 300 million years. They're eel-like but you can tell the difference because eels have jaws. Lampreys have a disc-like sucking mouth, bearing a complex arrangement of horny teeth inside. Now attached, the parasite will use its toothed tongue like a piston, to rasp away the scales and flesh of the sea trout. Then it will begin to feed on the trout's blood. Glands inside its head produce an anti-coagulant to ensure a continuous flow of blood. A larger lake trout could possibly survive this attack, but this lamprey is longer than its victim and will eventually drain all the vital fluids from its prey so that the trout dies.

This is an unnatural state of affairs since sea lampreys aren't natural born killers. In the ocean where they belong they usually take a blood meal without killing their host but in the Great Lakes their prey are smaller and can't survive a lamprey attack. Today, millions of dollars have to be spent controlling lampreys. To unravel the mystery of the land-locked sea lampreys, I went to the southern shore of Lake Huron in the state of Michigan in the USA.

The lake is vast and it stretched as far as I could see. As I walked along the beach the breeze whipped up waves as if I were looking at an ocean. I plunged my hand into the water to taste it – fresh, not saltwater. Between them the five Great Lakes – Huron, Michigan, Superior, Erie and Ontario – contain twenty per cent of all the world's surface freshwater. They also contain half a million or so sea lampreys but there used to be many more. As their name suggests, the fish shouldn't really be there at all and until the 1880s they weren't. Then man-made canals and shipping locks (which help the movement of boats) allowed their invasion to begin. At first they could only get into Lake Ontario – their route into the other lakes was blocked by the mighty Niagara Falls. Then – again, to help shipping – the Falls were bypassed by the Welland Canal, and by the 1930s the invaders were in all five of the Great Lakes.

Sea lampreys are like salmon, laying their eggs and spending the early stages of their lives in rivers, before migrating out to sea to mature and then running back upstream to spawn and die.

But the sea lampreys that colonized the Great Lakes didn't have to spend any time in the ocean; they had everything they needed in these huge bodies of freshwater, fed by innumerable streams. They were in lamprey heaven. There was so much food in the lake and the streams provided such good breeding sites that their population exploded and, by the 1940s, there were at least a million – perhaps several million – in each of the Lakes.

There are usually problems when plants and animals are in places where they don't belong and the sea lampreys were no exception. To prepare themselves for breeding, the adults must spend some time feeding on blood. In their natural state in the ocean these parasites usually latch on to shark-sized fish which can sustain the lamprey until they are just about full without coming to harm. But the fish in the Great Lakes – trout, white fish and chub – are considerably smaller, and losing blood to a feeding lamprey is often fatal. Each parasite can kill up to eighty-five kilograms of other fish before maturing. The bloodsuckers decimated the thriving fishery. The catch from the lakes was reduced from thirty-three million kilograms of lake trout, when the lakes were at their most productive, to only 66,000 kilograms after the lamprey population had exploded.

Something had to be done. Fishery scientists became vampire hunters. To film some of their methods we joined Roger Bergstedt and a colleague on the Trout River, a mile or so upstream before it joins Lake Huron. As we negotiated the base of the weir, Roger and his partner were sure-footed – they spend much of their time walking on slippery river rocks – especially from April to June when the lampreys are spawning. But I wasn't used to walking on slippery concrete covered with a sheet of fast flowing water. Inevitably it wasn't long before I fell backwards into the stream. Luckily the camera wasn't running so my fall wasn't filmed and I was wearing some waders that went right up to my chest – without them I'd have got a couple of bootfuls of water and wet, cold socks and feet. That's horrible.

On the second attempt I was filmed making

the crossing without mishap and we dragged a trap into the shallows. At one end there was a large entrance that got narrower and narrower, forming a funnel. So once the lampreys had worked their way inside the trap they got stuck and couldn't get out.

The captured lampreys made a racket and splashed water as they squirmed and writhed. I lifted the lid of the trap and plunged my hand inside. This was my first meeting with a sea lamprey in the flesh and it was very slippery flesh indeed. I just about managed to hold on so I could talk to the camera and show the lamprey's anatomy, but on a number of occasions I had to stop and start again as the slimy creatures wriggled from my grasp. Letting them suck on to the back of my hand seemed to calm them down but, once attached, their grip was tenacious and I really had to pull hard to get them off. Sometimes they made a round red mark on my skin and one even made me bleed with its teeth. The creatures in the trap were on their way upstream to spawn. Sea lampreys have a unique life cycle, which is also their downfall –

the breeding season is when scientists catch them. Trapping is one method, but there are others that are far more ingenious.

The next day I watched one of the ways scientists spoil a lamprey's chance of producing young as well as seeing another way the parasites use that sucker. Looking down from a bridge I could see light-coloured craters hollowed out of the river bed. Three or four lampreys wriggled in each one – these are fish that *make nests*. I took off my shoes and socks and waded into the stream and slowly approached a nest. Preoccupied with courtship, the lampreys took no notice even though one accidentally flicked my big toe with its tail.

The creatures were handling large pebbles, dragging them away from their nest depression with their sucker-like mouths. Beneath the dark stones there was a fine yellow gravel and that's why the nest craters stood out when I was looking down from the bridge. A stream bed with gravel is a perfect place for spawning, which is why the fish cleared away the larger rocks. 'Petromyzon' is the Latin name for sea lampreys, which means 'stone sucker'; watching them at work I could see why they are called this.

Looking through the crystal-clear water I watched a male frantically (and quite literally) keeping a close attachment to a female. Struggling against the current he worked his way along her body and secured his sucker to her head. But I could see a notch in his fins and knew his efforts would be in vain. Both lampreys thrashed their tails against the bottom, swirling up sand and sediment. They were releasing spawn and sperm, although none of the eggs would be fertilized.

The male had been nobbled by scientists on his way upstream. Taken to the Hammond Bay laboratory, he'd been injected with bisazir, a chemical that makes him infertile. The sterile male was marked by having one of his fins clipped. He was then released back into the river. I could see the notch in the fin once more as he left the female. They might come together many more times, but all they'd leave would be a nest of unfertilized eggs. Twenty-five thousand male lampreys are sterilized and released in the

Great Lakes every year. Sterilization plays an important role in the constant battle to control sea lampreys.

Not all migrating males can be captured, though, so some nests contain viable eggs. Once they hatch the vampire-hunters begin the second, and most deadly, phase of their attack. On hatching, the tiny, blind and toothless larvae migrate downstream from the spawning grounds and settle in areas of sandy silt. Even though they have no eyes, they can sense light with their tails – that's a crucial skill for the life that they'll lead. They are not vampires yet though. They live in burrows, hanging tail down, filtering debris and algae from the flowing water using a ring of filaments on the inside of their mouths which act as strainers.

If they stood on their heads in the burrow, their mouth would be away from food-laden currents, so a tail that's sensitive to light helps them keep the right way up. The baby lampreys are called ammocetes. They are so different from their parents that scientists first thought they were a separate species. They stay in their nurseries of silt for between three and seventeen years, growing to a length of fifteen centimetres. Then they become transformers, leaving the river and metamorphosing into parasitic adults that will suck the body fluids from other fish for between twelve and twenty months. That's unless the vampire-hunters get to their nurseries first.

Scientists from the American and Canadian Department of Fisheries treat 250 streams on a regular cycle. Any ammocetes in these are doomed. We filmed a stretch of river being cleared of lamprey larvae. White containers filled with a dark brown liquid were placed carefully on the river bank next to a small pump. A plastic tube perforated with holes was laid across the river and, when everything was ready, one end of the tube was put into the brown liquid and the pump turned on. The chemical was pumped at a steady rate into the stream. I could see the water becoming darker as the chemical issued from the holes in the tube and was washed downstream. The brown liquid is TFM, a lampricide (i.e. a substance that kills lampreys.) At the right concentration it's only lethal to lampreys, being harmless or having minimal side effects on other species of animals and plants including other kinds of fish. The cameraman put his camera in its waterproof housing and dunked it under the water next to a bank of sediment. He filmed the dead and dying ammocetes rising up from their tunnels in the mud, but the shoals of silvery minnows that flashed in the sunlight seemed completely unaffected by the lampricide in the water.

Barriers across the river are another way that lampreys can be prevented from reaching their nesting sites. We drove across the bridge that links the United States to Canada to film a lamprey barrier on a Canadian stream. This particular barrier was called an adjustable crest barrier. It is only inflated during sea lamprey spawning runs so for the rest of the year other fish can pass upstream unhindered. It's controlled by a computer in the nearby town of Sault Ste Marie. The computer automatically adjusts the barrier height according to the water levels at the time, so alterations to the river's natural flow are minimized.

Another barrier – the low-head type – relies on the fact that lampreys are poor jumpers compared with salmon and trout. A 60–120cm drop is enough to stop lampreys. If there's a water-jumping pool below the structure, the other fish can clear it easily. Sometimes these barriers have a lip otherwise the lampreys may use their suction mouths to climb over it.

All in all, millions of dollars are spent every year in the battle against sea lampreys. I feel quite sorry for all the sea lampreys that die but the land-locked lamprey is very destructive and if the vampire-killing scientists stopped their work in the Great Lakes, lamprey numbers would explode once again and the trout, white fish and chub that truly belong there would be decimated.

On our last day I couldn't resist a dip in the chilly waters of Lake Huron. The cold took my breath away, but I was determined to swim fifty metres out and then turn and come back. At the farthest point out from the shore, I thought I felt something on the side of my body. Back in the shallows I stood up – a lamprey had hitched a ride with me. Looking at it actually attached to my flesh underlined how bizarre these creatures are – the slimy body glistening in the sunlight, the black hole on the top of its head (its single nostril) and that round mouth sucking at my skin. You don't get creatures much weirder than sea lampreys!

The fish didn't hang on for long. Thankfully it sensed I was warm-blooded and not a giant trout. That was six months ago, but I still have nightmares about lampreys attacking humans. Just imagine one boring into your flesh and sucking your life-giving blood away!

## Lampreys – Fact Box

● Lampreys aren't the only fish that feed on blood. In South America there are tiny catfish called Candiru. They swim into the gill openings of other fish and gorge on blood from the gills. They have also been known to swim into humans, particularly if they're relieving themselves in the water. Once inside, their spines cause excruciating pain and can only be removed by surgery.

● Lampreys are the only type of fish, other than sharks, to have electro-receptors which they use to detect the tiny pulses of electricity produced by the heart and muscles of their prey.

● Lampreys have only one nostril and that's on the top of their heads.

# Mosquitoes:
# The Ultimate Vampires

There is a vampire that at one time or another most of us have been bitten by. In fact the majority of humans that have ever lived have been bitten by this bloodsucker. It was sucking the blood of the dinosaurs and was ready to make flying visits to us when we evolved about a million years ago. At the very least these vampires are an annoying nuisance. At worst they bring sickness and death. They're disliked more than just about any other animal and they're the most dangerous creature on earth.

I'm describing, of course, that group of biting flies – there's about 3,500 species in all – which we call mosquitoes. I first came across them in big numbers when I was fifteen and on a hunt for reptiles and amphibians in the Carmargue, a huge marsh at the delta of the Rhone river in southern France. At the end of my first day there was a glorious sunset. I heard a sound like honking geese and my breath was taken away by flocks of flamingos flying to their roosts. The vivid pink birds were almost camouflaged against a sky turned red by the setting sun.

But my exhilaration was short-lived. The honks of the flamingos were replaced by a high-pitched whine that became louder and louder as if it came from inside my head – but I wasn't imagining anything. Clouds of mosquitoes dipped and dived all around me and I fancied I could feel their delicate touch as they landed on my face and arms. I must admit I panicked and walked as fast as I could back the way I thought I'd come – except it wasn't and I was lost in a mosquito-infested swamp. Taking deep breaths I racked my brain for landmarks, trying to keep calm and not run. Eventually I found my way to the main road where I'd got off the bus from Arles, the main town, earlier that day.

Back at the hostel I looked in the mirror. My face was ghastly: the flesh was puffy and inflated and the bumps surrounding each mosquito bite were so swollen my head was like a mountain range with shallow, narrow valleys between each peak. I couldn't sleep that night, the irritation was so intense, and I couldn't stop scratching.

The mosquito's bite isn't toxic but in their saliva there are four proteins which initiate an allergic response. The first time ever that a person is bitten nothing will happen and they won't notice anything at all. But the next time they are bitten they'll be sensitized and the classic itchy raised bump will develop. The Carmargue was probably one of the first ten times I'd been so badly bitten and my body's allergic response was severe. Thankfully this lessens with time and now my skin barely raises a bump when I'm bitten; if it does, the irritation rarely lasts longer than an hour or so. I'm overjoyed by this as my job would be a misery if I had a similar reaction to the one I had in the Carmargue every time I was bitten. I often travel in the tropics and the Arctic tundra, parts of the world that are mosquito heaven.

Seventy-five per cent of all mosquito species live in the tropics. Because of the constant warmth there, and the many different habitats, there can be 150 species in a square mile. There are fewer species in the Arctic but the ones that are there occur in phenomenal densities: hordes of them can literally blacken the sky. I saw this vampire spectacular in Coujaac in Quebec, Canada when we were filming the migration of caribou (called reindeer in Europe). The first clue came when I looked out of my motel window and noticed the local people seemed to be ultra-friendly – every few seconds they were waving at somebody. But when I went outside I realized the Coujaac wave was a way of brushing away mosquitoes that constantly hover in front of your face.

The swarms could be outrun – most mosquitoes only fly at about one kilometre an hour – but when we had to be still because of filming the nervous caribou herds or a golden eagle at its nest, we wore a full suit of netting and hats with nets to cover our face to keep the mosquitoes from biting. We soaked the netting in repellent. Surprisingly, the chemicals used in mosquito sprays don't so much repel mosquitoes as just disguise our attractiveness as a host for a blood meal.

Mosquitoes have refined finding their hosts to an extraordinary degree. When you think about it, they've had to. Many species set out in total darkness to find prey. These tiny flying machines home in on the warm air and carbon dioxide in the exhaled breath of their host. They steer a course upwind, zigzagging back and forth in the stream of warm carbon dioxide-rich air. Once they're close, the mosquitoes zoom in on their target using temperature, humidity, colours and chemicals that emanate from the skin. Some individual humans are much more attractive to mosquitoes than others. Some people seem to be not bitten at all, presumably because of individual differences in skin chemistry. Some mosquitoes are choosy about what part of the body they extract blood from. If scientists bait traps with Limburger cheese – a particularly 'stinky' variety – they catch significantly higher numbers of certain mosquito species which are also notorious ankle biters. It's perhaps not a coincidence that the same bacteria that produce the smell in feet are closely related to the ones that make cheese pong! And these mosquito species are attracted to both.

The mosquitoes of the Arctic are only on the wing during the brief Arctic summer, but during that time they seem to be active twenty-four hours a day. If they were creatures of the night, like many other mosquitoes they'd be in trouble, because in the high Arctic in summer the sun never actually sets, so it's light all the time!

The day-flying Coujuac mosquitoes gave me an opportunity to satisfy my scientific curiosity and find out how mosquitoes bite and breed. I didn't, however, go to the extremes of the scientists who sat on the tundra without their shirts to gauge the attack-rate of North Canadian mosquitoes. Incredibly, they suffered

289 bites per minute on their arms. That would have meant 9,000 bites per minute over the whole body if they'd been completely naked. At that rate they would have lost half of their blood in just two hours.

I was just brave enough to expose my hand so I could watch a mosquito biting. As soon as the insect had landed it moved its mouthparts over my skin and then it began to cut through my flesh. I could only see the sheath that encloses the mouth parts. Inside that there was a tube for sucking my blood, another for injecting saliva and others for piercing and cutting my flesh. I didn't feel a thing as the mouth parts disappeared into me. The tip would now be scanning for blood just beneath the surface. Once blood was located, the serrated mouth parts would saw back and forth through my tissue, lacerating small capillaries. The feeding tube would now be injected into the pool of blood that forms, and pumps in the head would begin to suck up the meal. The mosquito's abdomen swelled as I watched. This was fascinating – really! – even though my blood was the beverage the insect was drinking. Then a perfect sphere of red liquid formed at its back end. The mosquito was getting rid of the watery part of my blood, so it could pack in more red blood cells (the nutritious part). At the end of the meal it would be twice its own weight. I'd provided this mosquito with about five millionths of a litre of Marven blood.

Forty-five seconds after it had alighted the mosquito was airborne; about a minute after that, there was a white lump on my skin which itched. That's why mosquitoes must work fast to penetrate the skin and tap blood. The allergic reaction to the saliva could warn their prey that they're there and that means they're likely to be squashed. If they feed quickly, by the time the host knows something is amiss, it's too late.

I knew that I'd just provided lunch for a female mosquito because males don't drink blood. Both sexes get much of their energy from drinking the sugar nectar of plants. In fact, here, in the Arctic, many orchids rely on them for pollination. Nectar is adequate for males but, to develop eggs, females need a more nutritious juice: blood.

The main reason mosquitoes are a scourge in the Arctic is because water can't percolate away through the ground (which has a permanently frozen layer – the permafrost). Above the permafrost a network of shallow pools forms, and each pool is a perfect nursery for mosquitoes, which lay their eggs in water. These hatch into larvae which are sometimes found in millions. I can vouch for this myself. Whenever I loomed above any pool near Coujuac it seethed as mosquito larvae frantically thrashed their tails, propelling themselves underwater just in case I was a predator. If I stayed still, they'd gradually float back up to the surface. There they'd lay, breathing with waterproof siphons that they push through the surface film into the air above. The larvae don't have gills like fish and would drown if they were held under for long.

Their tiny bodies are covered in bristles which have a dual function. The ones on the body help keep them afloat while the ones in front of the jet black eyes are used for feeding. There are about a thousand of them arranged in a brush-like structure on either side of the head. These bristles make rhythmic sweeping movements which draw in water currents laden with tiny particles of food to the mouth.

Intermingled with the larvae there was the next stage in the life cycle. These creatures reminded me of 3-D mobile commas or, more fancifully, miniature skulls that can swim. These were the pupae of the mosquitoes. These are equivalent to the chrysalises of butterflies except mosquito pupae are highly mobile. When my shadow fell on them they dashed through the water by making kicking movements with their abdomens which have a large paddle at the end.

Floating in the breeze on the pool's surface I could see some brown husks. These were the empty cases of pupae from which adult mosquitoes had hatched. I still marvel at these insect transformations, whether it be a mosquito, a butterfly, or a dragonfly. In all these cases a legless larvae that does little but feed, converts into a long, slender-legged flying machine. For sheer strangeness and improbability these transformations far exceed the wildest flights of our imagination.

But in the mosquito's case, this awe and wonderment is tempered by the fact that on a flying visit to us these ultimate vampires can inject a deadly load. A mosquito drooling its saliva into you during a bite can be a prelude to sickness and death. Dengue, yellow, and Ross River fever are a few of the 100 or so viral diseases injected by mosquitoes. The insects can also transmit parasitic worms (filariasis is one of the most serious of these) and protozoa (one-celled) parasites (plasmodium is one of these, the cause of malaria).

Thankfully, mosquitoes are not carriers of the HIV virus that causes AIDS because they can't be infected with it themselves. For mosquitoes, the HIV virus is just part of the meal and is killed and broken down in the mosquito's gut. They never carry pathogens (agents that cause disease) directly from the blood of the victim to another because their bite is so precise – there is no blood on the outside of their mouthparts that could be smeared on to the next person they bite. They can only spread diseases that they are susceptible to themselves. The pathogen will infect their gut and from there be passed into the salivary glands. Once there the pathogen can be injected into a new host during feeding. The mosquito can be infectious for the rest of its life (perhaps another week or two) during which time it may pass on pathogens at three or four more feeds.

For humans, fighting mosquitoes and the organisms they carry in their spit, is an on-going war. We win one battle and lose another; we attack, and then the insects and parasites evolve new countermeasures. The mosquito may even leave one battlefield and start up another. The amazing ability of the mosquito to adapt to changing environments led me to visit an immense pile of tyres in Baltimore, Maryland.

We wanted to show how mosquitoes can immigrate in the most surprising ways. Until 1985 the tiger mosquito was unknown in the Western Hemisphere. Then it was imported into Texas, probably with a shipment of used tyres from Japan. The handsome insect gets its name from bold black and white stripes. It also bites in full sunshine, so it didn't stay unnoticed for long.

Soon it had spread over much of the Eastern United States. In Asia it transmits serious diseases, so American scientists had to plan a counterattack. Before control teams are sent in to an area, inspectors do a test, one which I helped them with. Standing still, wearing dark clothes (mosquitoes seem to prefer these), I had to count how many females landed on me in an allotted amount of time. More than five in a minute indicated pest control was needed. Near the mountain of rubber tyres in Baltimore I was attacked fifteen times in one minute. The tiger control teams moved in in a big way!

The tyres were part of the problem. Tiger mosquitoes are known as container breeders, which means their larvae can grow and develop in any man-made objects that hold water: anything from butts to bird baths and water bowls for pets. Tyres that are stored outside make a perfect breeding place – as when stacked or stored nearly all of them contain some water. In the United States there are four billion tyres – four billion potential breeding places for tiger mosquitoes. These tyres also provide the insects with transportation: tyres that are going to be remade into other rubber products – gaskets, washers and the like – are traded and stored outdoors before being shipped long distances. Mosquito eggs laid, for example, in a tyre in Houston can hatch 800 kilometres away. To control the tiger mosquito there is a desperate need to eliminate any water-filled nurseries for their young. Public co-operation is needed to keep them at bay.

Mosquitoes and other parasites have always been with us and probably always will be. As carriers of disease, they've been responsible for more human deaths than any other animal. Malaria has killed hundreds of millions of people, mainly in the tropics. Two hundred million people are suffering from malaria today and some 100 million new cases occur each year. Probably one million people, mostly children, die from malaria annually.

In the past – during the age of exploration, for instance – mosquito-borne diseases stopped hunters and colonists dead in their tracks. On Sir Francis Drake's expedition in 1585, hundreds of men died, probably from mosquito-borne yellow fever picked up in the Cape Verde Islands west of Africa. In 1802 the brother-in-law of Napoleon, Charles Lecherc, lost 29,000 of his 33,000-strong force to the same disease. At the beginning of this century France spent millions of francs in its attempts to build the Panama Canal, but disease-carrying mosquitoes defeated them. In 1902 the United States took over the project. Their health officials realized how serious an enemy mosquitoes were and enforced stringent control regulations; at last the canal could be completed.

But what does the future hold for relations between mosquitoes and humans? The war is still being waged and the area of the world that this war covers is expanding. Because of global warming the mosquitoes that carry deadly diseases are spreading north. Malaria-carrying mosquitoes are a rarity in temperate regions but they could become commonplace. The bird baths and paddling pools in British gardens may one day be nurseries for some of the fifty or so mosquito species that transmit malaria.

As long as we're around as unwitting donors of blood, mosquitoes – the ultimate vampires – will whine around our heads before darting towards their prey to feed. Of course, that's unless the blood-thirsty marauder is flattened by a slap of the hand first!

# Mosquitoes – Fact Box

● Mosquitoes take an involuntary blood donation from us even though they're a millionth of our size.

● Every thirty seconds a child in Africa dies of malaria, a disease that can only be transmitted by the bite of a mosquito.

● Forty per cent of the world's human population live in areas where they are at risk from the disease. That percentage is increasing as global warming takes malaria into areas that were once too cold.

● Only female mosquitoes suck blood, the males feed on fruit juice and nectar from flowers.

● Unwashed human feet and Limburger cheese both have a pungent odour and both nourish bacteria that produce a substance attractive to mosquitoes.